PUTTING THE PARTY IN POLITICAL PARTIES

Our Candidate Won't Sling Mud

"The Things They Whisper Ain't as Bad as What They Shout Out Loud" by

WILL ROGERS

VIRGINIA LOH-HAGAN

45TH PARALLEL PRESS

Published in the United States of America by Cherry Lake Publishing Group
Ann Arbor, Michigan
www.cherrylakepublishing.com

Reading Adviser: Beth Walker Gambro, MS, Ed., Reading Consultant, Yorkville, IL
Content Adviser: Mark Richards, Ph.D., Professor, Dept. of Political Science, Grand Valley State
University, Allendale, MI
Book Designer: Frame25 Productions

Photo Credits: Life Magazine, TIME Incorporated, Internet Archive, Public Domain, cover, title page;
© Blulz60/Shutterstock, 5; © PeskyMonkey/Shutterstock, 7; Life Magazine, TIME Incorporated,
Internet Archive, Public Domain, 11; CBS TelevisionUploaded by We hope at en.wikipedia, Public
domain, via Wikimedia Commons, 13; © Jeffrey M. Frank/Shutterstock, 17; Jonathon Sharkey, CC
BY-SA 3.0 via Wikimedia Commons, 19; Massachusetts Pirate Party, CC0, via Wikimedia Commons,
21; David Shankbone, CC BY 3.0 via Wikimedia Commons, 25; © vesperstock/Shutterstock, 29; © Lisa
F. Young/Shutterstock, 31

45th Parallel Press is an imprint of Cherry Lake Publishing Group.

Library of Congress Cataloging-in-Publication Data has been filed and is available at catalog.loc.gov

Cherry Lake Publishing Group would like to acknowledge the work of the Partnership for 21st
Century Learning, a Network of Battelle for Kids. Please visit Battelle for Kids online for more
information.

Note from publisher: Websites change regularly, and their future contents are outside of our
control. Supervise children when conducting any recommended online searches for extended
learning opportunities.

Printed in the United States of America

ABOUT THE AUTHOR

Dr. Virginia Loh-Hagan is an author and educator. She is currently the Director of the Asian Pacific
Islander Desi American (APIDA) Center at San Diego State University and the Co-Executive Director
of The Asian American Education Project. She lives in San Diego with her very tall husband and very
naughty dogs.

CONTENTS

Introduction 4

Chapter 1: **High Moral Party** 8

Chapter 2: **Anti-Bunk Party** 10

Chapter 3: **Surprise Party** 12

Chapter 4: **American Vegetarian Party** 14

Chapter 5: **OWL Party of Washington** 16

Chapter 6: **Vampires, Witches, and Pagans Party** 18

Chapter 7: **United States Pirate Party** 20

Chapter 8: **Objectivist Party** 22

Chapter 9: **"The Rent is 2 Damn High" Party** 24

Chapter 10: **Breakfast-All-Day Party** 26

Do Your Part! 28

Glossary, Learn More, Index 32

INTRODUCTION

The United States is a top world power. It's not ruled by kings or queens. It's a **democracy**. A democracy is a system of government. It means "rule by the people." People **elect** their leaders. They choose leaders by voting.

Leaders **represent** the people who voted for them. They speak for them. They make decisions for them. That's why voting is so important. By voting, we choose our leaders.

Candidates run for **public office**. Public office is a government position. Candidates work hard to get votes. They run **campaigns**. They do this before an election. Campaigns are planned activities. Some campaigns are easy. Some are hard. And some are full of drama.

From local to federal, every candidate
running for public office has a campaign.

Political parties are groups. They organize campaigns. They support a candidate. They raise money. They host events. They vote. They help candidates win. Political parties have members. These members share the same beliefs. They share the same goals.

The United States has two main parties. The Republican Party is traditional. They think government should play a small part in people's lives. The Democratic Party supports progress. They think government should do more to help people. Both parties believe in democracy.

Some political parties are big. Some are small. Some support issues. Some are silly. U.S. history is full of political parties. This book features some of the fun ones!

The U.S. has a multi-party system. But 2 political parties hold most of the power.

CHAPTER ONE

HIGH MORAL PARTY

Leonard Jones (1797–1868) was from Kentucky. He joined several religious groups. He also loved running for office. He ran for Congress. He even ran for U.S. president. He did this several times from the 1840s to the 1860s.

Jones was popular. Crowds followed him. He gave speeches. He yelled. He jumped around. He waved a cane. He pounded it on tables. He said **moral** people would live forever. Moral means good. It means knowing right from wrong. Jones started a "live forever" religion. He said sin caused sickness and death. He founded the High Moral Party. He was the only member.

But Jones didn't live forever. He died in his sleep.

WORLD AFFAIRS

Other countries have political parties. The Church of the Militant Elvis Party was formed in 2001. It's a political party in the United Kingdom. The party is focused on climate change. It's focused on saving the Amazon rainforests. It's focused on decreasing the power of big companies.

David Bishop (1944–2022) was its leader. He ran in more than a dozen elections. He called himself "Lord Biro." This is after the English poet Lord Byron (1788–1824). Bishop was also known as "Bus-pass Elvis." He dressed as Elvis Presley (1935–1977). Presley was an American singer. He's known as the "King of Rock and Roll." Bishop said voters liked the Elvis image. His campaign is silly. He said, "Some of it is obviously a joke. But I like raising issues other people don't campaign on."

CHAPTER TWO

ANTI-BUNK PARTY

Will Rogers (1879–1935) was a famous entertainer. He was known for his sense of humor. He was from Oklahoma. He traveled around the world. He made 71 movies. He was on radio shows. He wrote more than 4,000 newspaper articles.

Rogers wrote for *Life* magazine. He made fun of politics. He said, "I don't make jokes. I just watch the government and report the facts."

He thought campaigning was **bunk**. Bunk means silly or fake. To prove this point, he ran for U.S. president. He did this in 1928. He wrote weekly articles in *Life*. He called himself the "bunkless candidate." He ran for the Anti-Bunk Party. It was a fake campaign. But he got a lot of attention.

The Anti-Bunk Party was a joke.
Life magazine had many articles about it.

CHAPTER THREE
SURPRISE PARTY

Gracie Allen (1895–1964) was a performer. She worked with her husband. He was George Burns (1896–1996). They were a comedy team. They performed on radio, TV, and movies.

Burns and Allen played pranks. They did this to promote their shows. In 1940, they ran a fake campaign. Allen said she was running for president. She and Burns traveled across the country. They went to more than 30 cities. They did live radio shows.

Their political party was the Surprise Party. Their **mascot** was the kangaroo. Mascots are symbols. The Surprise Party **slogan** was "It's in the bag." A slogan is a catchy phrase.

Allen and Burns were popular. It's well-known that many Harvard students pledged their vote to Allen.

CHAPTER FOUR

AMERICAN VEGETARIAN PARTY

Vegetarians don't eat meat. But they do run for office! The American Vegetarian Party formed in 1947. It promoted a meatless lifestyle. Symon Gould (1894–1963) and Dr. John Maxwell (1864–1963) founded the party. Gould co-edited the *American Vegetarian* magazine. Maxwell owned a vegetarian restaurant. He said he hadn't tasted meat in 45 years.

In 1947, about 500 people met. They met at a hotel in New York. They picked their first candidate. They chose Maxwell for the 1948 presidential election. But he was born in England. So he was not allowed to run. Gould was the 1960 and 1964 candidate for the party.

THE IDEAL CANDIDATE

Ideal candidates are role models. Some political parties are shady. But many try to do good work. The best political parties are formed by the people. The Aloha ʻĀina Party of Hawaii was formed in 1997. It means "love of the land." It promotes the needs of Native Hawaiians. It fights to promote Hawaiian culture. It fights to preserve Hawaiian history. It fights for Hawaiian sovereignty. Sovereignty is the right to govern itself. The Aloha ʻĀina Party of Hawaii rejects the U.S. overthrow of their queen in 1893. Queen Liliʻuokalani (1838–1917) inspired the party. She once said, "Do not be afraid. Be steadfast in aloha for your land and people." The party wants more Hawaiians to vote. It wants more Native Hawaiians in office. They practice hoʻoponopono. This means "making right what is wrong." They believe in Mālama ʻĀina. This means "taking care of the land." They also believe in Aloha Kānaka. This means "love for the people."

CHAPTER FIVE

OWL PARTY OF WASHINGTON

Red Kelly (1927–2004) owned a jazz club. The jazz club was in Tumwater, Washington. By 1976, Kelly's club was a popular spot for **politicians**. Politicians are elected to public office.

One night, Kelly and his friends were hanging out. They decided to run for office. Some ran with funny nicknames. Kelly ran for Washington state governor.

The group created the OWL Party. OWL stood for "Out With **Logic**." It also stood for "On With **Lunacy**." Logic means reason. Lunacy means insanity. The slogan was "We don't give a hoot." Their campaign was a joke. But they still got about 250,000 votes.

The state of Washington didn't think the OWL Party was funny. It changed its laws. It made new rules for how political parties could be formed.

CHAPTER SIX

VAMPIRES, WITCHES, AND PAGANS PARTY

Jonathon Sharkey (born 1964) is a former professional wrestler. But he's more famous for claiming to be a vampire. He says he first drank blood at age five. He tried to create a town of vampires in Tennessee.

Sharkey likes running for office. He ran for U.S. president in 2004 and 2008. He ran for Congress several times. He also ran for governor of Minnesota. He says he's different from most politicians. He said he doesn't hide his evil side.

He ran for the Vampires, Witches, and **Pagans** Party. Pagans worship many gods. They worship nature. They don't follow traditional religions.

Sharkey doesn't believe in God. He believes in the devil. He thinks the devil led a rebellion against harsh and unfair government.

CHAPTER SEVEN

UNITED STATES PIRATE PARTY

The United States Pirate Party (USPP) was founded in 2006. It's part of the International Pirate Movement. Pirate parties support civil rights. They support free sharing of knowledge. They support free speech. They support the protection of privacy. The USPP focuses on how information is shared on the internet.

Its name refers to **piracy**. Piracy means using others' work without permission. But the party also uses pirate themes. An example is the members' names. The leader of the Pirate Party is a "captain." Their slogan is "No safe harbor for the enemies of liberty." Their logo is a pirate ship flag.

The USPP has more than 3,000 members. It has more than 7 state chapters. Several USPP members have run for office.

The first Pirate Party started in Sweden. It started in 2006.
There are more than 29 Pirate Parties around the world.

CHAPTER EIGHT

OBJECTIVIST PARTY

Thomas Stevens (1956–2019) was a lawyer. He founded the Objectivist Party on February 2, 2008. He founded it on Ayn Rand's (1905–1982) birthday. Rand was a writer. She believed in objectivism. Objectivism values reason. It values self-interest. It values personal freedom. It values one's happiness above all.

In 2009, Stevens went to New York. He visited Rand's grave. He made a speech there. He thanked Rand for bringing objectivism to the world. He said others need to help spread it.

The Objectivist Party held its first **convention** in 2010. Conventions are large meetings. Stevens was the party leader. He was the party candidate. He ran for U.S. president in 2012.

HOT-BUTTON ISSUE

Hot-button issues refer to tough topics. People have strong emotions. They take sides. Political parties started forming in the 1790s. U.S. Presidents George Washington (1732–1799) and Thomas Jefferson (1743–1826) pushed policies. Parties formed in favor of or against these policies. Today, the party system is much more powerful. One hot-button issue is whether political parties should exist. Some people think political parties cause tensions and divide people. They split votes. They split control. Some people vote along party lines. They vote for the party's candidate, no matter what. Others think people should vote based on issues. They want voters to support the best candidates. They want to get rid of political parties. There's another point of view. Some people value political parties. They think they're good for democracy. Political parties force people to compromise. They provide checks and balances. They push people to ask questions. They promote diverse thinking. They also support community.

CHAPTER NINE

"THE RENT IS 2 DAMN HIGH" PARTY

Jimmy McMillan III (born 1946) is from New York City. He runs for office a lot. He ran for mayor. He ran for governor. But he hasn't won any elections. He founded "The Rent Is 2 Damn High" Party. He used *damn* on purpose. He did it to shock people. He said the words in a **debate**. Debates are discussions about topics. McMillan's famous words became **viral**. Viral means spreading quickly.

McMillan's party focuses on one issue. It is the high rent in New York City. The party's slogan is "breakfast, lunch, and dinner." It aims to end hunger and poverty.

McMillan said, "My job was to try to use my entertaining ability to get people to pay attention."

CHAPTER TEN

BREAKFAST-ALL-DAY PARTY

Dean Greco is from New Jersey. He teaches social studies. He works at a middle school. He ran for Congress. He did this in 2008. He created his own political party. His party was called the Breakfast-All-Day Party.

Nicole Greco is his wife. She is a reporter. She made a film about her husband's campaign. She wanted to show how the political system worked. The film is called "100 Signatures." Her husband needed 100 signatures to run for office. He narrates the film. He's also in it as a candidate.

The Grecos hosted a party. They showed the film. They served breakfast.

FACT-CHECK

It's important to check facts. Facts must be correct. Here are some fun facts about political parties:

- The Democratic Party is older than the Republican Party. Andrew Jackson (1767–1845) was the first Democratic president. Abraham Lincoln (1809–1865) was the first Republican president. The Republican Party formed to stop the spread of slavery.

- The Know-Nothings Party or Know-Nothing Party formed in the 1840s. Party members were against immigration. They wanted the Bible to be read in schools. They were a secret society. They had passwords. They had hand signs. When asked about the party, they had to say, "I know nothing."

- The U.S. Green Party formed in the 1980s. It's focused on saving the planet. It's focused on peace. It's anti-war. There are green parties around the world. They exist in more than 90 countries.

- The world's top 2 largest political parties are in Asia. India's Bharatiya Janata Party (BJP) is the largest political party. It has about 180 million members. The 2nd largest is the Chinese Communist Party (CCP). It has about 98 million members.

DO YOUR PART!

U.S. citizens have 2 special rights. Only U.S. citizens can vote in federal elections. Only U.S. citizens can run for **federal office**. Federal office means a national office. It's different from state and local offices.

U.S. citizens have many other rights. But they also have duties. The most powerful is the duty to vote. Voting is how people choose leaders. It's how people make changes. It's how people promote their ideas. Those elected make the laws. They make policies. They make the rules. They work for voters.

U.S. citizens can vote at age 18. But people are never too young to get involved in democracy.

U.S. citizens take pride in being able to vote for their leaders.

Citizens have to sign up to vote. They can choose a political party. They can also choose "no party." Here are some ideas to learn more about political parties:

★ Volunteer for a local election. Work with candidates from different parties. See how they work. Learn more about their ideas.

★ Go online. Research different parties. Make a list of things you like. Make a list of things you don't like. Do this for each party.

★ Interview members of political parties. Ask them why they joined their parties.

Everyone can do their part. Being a good citizen is hard work. But the work is worth it. Your vote is your voice.

You can volunteer to assist with elections. This will help you learn more about the election process.

GLOSSARY

bunk (BUNK) something that is silly or untrue

campaigns (kam-PAYNZ) organized courses of action to achieve a goal such as winning an election

candidates (KAN-duh-dayts) people who want to be elected to certain positions

convention (kuhn-VEN-shun) an assembly of people meeting for a common purpose

debate (dih-BAYT) a formal discussion between two people or groups on an important subject

democracy (dih-MAH-kruh-see) a system of government led by voters, often through elected representatives

elect (ih-LEKT) to choose someone to hold public office by voting

federal office (FEH-druhl AW-fuhs) an elected position in the national government

logic (LAH-jik) reason

lunacy (LOO-nuh-see) extreme foolishness or insanity

mascot (MAA-skaht) a person, animal, or object that symbolizes a group

moral (MOHR-uhl) relating to the principles of right and wrong

pagans (PAY-gunz) people who worship nature and/or many gods

piracy (PYE-rah-see) using content created by other people without permission

political parties (puh-LIH-tuh-kuhl PAR-teez) organized groups of people who have similar political ideas

politicians (pah-luh-TIH-shunz) people who hold elected offices

public office (PUH-blik AW-fuhs) government position established by law

represent (reh-prih-ZENT) to speak or act for another person or group

slogan (SLOH-guhn) a short, memorable phrase used in advertising

vegetarians (veh-juh-TAIR-ee-uhns) people who do not eat meat

LEARN MORE

Books

Burgan, Michael. *Political Parties*. North Mankato: Capstone Press, 2008.

Meister, Cari. *Political Parties: A Kid's Guide*. North Mankato: Capstone Press, 2020.

Weber, M. *Political Parties*. Parker, CO: The Child's World, 2020.

INDEX

Allen, Gracie, 12–13
Aloha 'Āina Party of Hawaii, 15
American Vegetarian Party, 14
Anti-Bunk Party, 10–11

Bishop, David, 9
Breakfast-All-Day Party, 26
Burns, George, 12–13

candidates, 4–5, 6
Church of the Militant Elvis Party, 9
comedians, 10–11, 12–13

democracy, 4, 6, 23, 28–31
Democratic Party, 6, 27

environmental values, 9, 14, 15, 27

Gould, Symon, 14
Green Party, 27

gubernatorial elections, 16, 18, 24

Hawaii, 15
High Moral Party, 8

Jackson, Andrew, 27
Jefferson, Thomas, 23
joke campaigns, 10–11, 12, 16
Jones, Leonard, 8

Kelly, Red, 16
Know-Nothings Party, 27

Lili'uokalani of Hawaii, 15
Lincoln, Abraham, 27

Maxwell, John, 14
McMillan, Jimmy, III, 24–25

Objectivist Party, 22
OWL Party, 16–17

Pirate Party, 20–21
political parties, 6, 23, 27
    formation rules, 17
    systems, 6, 7, 23
poverty issues, 24–25
privacy values, 20

"The Rent Is 2 Damn High" Party, 24–25
Republican Party, 6, 27
Rogers, Will, 10–11

Sharkey, Jonathon, 18–19
Stevens, Thomas, 22
Surprise Party, 12–13

Vampires, Witches, and Pagans Party, 18–19
voting and voting rights, 4, 23, 28–31

Washington, George, 23